TALES OF INVENTI

THE SUBMARINE

Richard and Louise Spilsbury

Raintree is an imprint of Capstone Global Library Limited, a company incorporated in England and Wales having its registered office at 7 Pilgrim Street, London, EC4V 6LB – Registered company number: 6695582

www.raintreepublishers.co.uk
myorders@raintreepublishers.co.uk

Text © Capstone Global Library Limited 2011
First published in hardback in 2011
Published in paperback in 2012
The moral rights of the proprietor have been asserted.

All rights reserved. No part of this publication may be reproduced in any form or by any means (including photocopying or storing it in any medium by electronic means and whether or not transiently or incidentally to some other use of this publication) without the written permission of the copyright owner, except in accordance with the provisions of the Copyright, Designs and Patents Act 1988 or under the terms of a licence issued by the Copyright Licensing Agency, Saffron House, 6–10 Kirby Street, London EC1N 8TS (www.cla.co.uk). Applications for the copyright owner's written permission should be addressed to the publisher.

Edited by Louise Galpine and Laura Knowles
Designed by Philippa Jenkins
Original illustrations © Capstone Global Library Ltd 2011
Illustrated by KJA-artists.com
Picture research by Mica Brancic
Originated by Capstone Global Library Ltd
Printed and bound in Dubai

ISBN 978-1-4062-8879-7 (paperback)
18 17 16 15 14
10 9 8 7 6 5 4 3 2 1

British Library Cataloguing in Publication Data
Spilsbury, Louise.
The submarine. -- (Tales of invention)
623.8'205'09-dc22
A full catalogue record for this book is available from the British Library.

Acknowledgements
We would like to thank the following for permission to reproduce photographs: Alamy pp. **6** (© LondonPhotos - Homer Sykes), **17** (© Tara Carlin); Corbis pp. **19** (© Bettmann), **23** (© Bettmann); Getty Images pp. **5** (MPI/Hulton Archive), **11** (MPI/Hulton Archive), **12** (De Agostini), **13** (Stock Montage/Hulton Archive), **15** (Hulton Archive), **21** (National Geographic/Emory Kristof), **22** (National Geographic/Emory Kristof), **26** (Photo by BAE Systems), **27**; iStockphoto p. **4** (© Christophe Schmid); © Mary Evans Picture Library 2007 p. **8**; NavSource Naval History p. **18** (US Navy photo courtesy of Darryl Baker. Negative scanned courtesy of By Design, Benicia, CA); NOAA p. **25** (Institute for Exploration/University of Rhode Island); Photolibrary pp. **10** (North Wind Picture Archives), **20** (Brand X Pictures); Rex Features p. **7** (Roger-Viollet); www.navy.mil p. **14** (US Navy, Chief of Naval Operations Submarine Warfare Division (N87)).

Cover photograph of John P. Holland standing in the conning tower of his submarine, *Holland VI*, April 1898, Perth Amboy, New Jersey, USA, reproduced with permission of Corbis/© Bettmann.

We would like to thank Ian Graham for his invaluable help in the preparation of this book.

Every effort has been made to contact copyright holders of material reproduced in this book. Any omissions will be rectified in subsequent printings if notice is given to the publisher.

Disclaimer
All the Internet addresses (URLs) given in this book were valid at the time of going to press. However, due to the dynamic nature of the Internet, some addresses may have changed, or sites may have changed or ceased to exist since publication. While the author and publisher regret any inconvenience this may cause readers, no responsibility for any such changes can be accepted by either the author or the publisher.

NORFOLK LIBRARIES & INFORMATION SERVICE	
1526230	
PETERS	09-Oct-2014
623.82	£7.99
PBK	

CONTENTS

Look for these boxes

BEFORE SUBMARINES 4
THE FIRST SUBMARINES 6
IMPROVING SUBMARINES 12
SUBMARINES WITH ENGINES. . . 16
EXPLORING THE OCEANS 22
INTO THE FUTURE 26
TIMELINE 28
GLOSSARY. 30
FIND OUT MORE 31
INDEX. 32

Biographies
These boxes tell you about the life of inventors, the dates when they lived, and their important discoveries.

Setbacks

Here we tell you about the experiments that didn't work, the failures, and the accidents.

EUREKA!
These boxes tell you about important events and discoveries, and what inspired them.

Any words appearing in the text in bold, **like this**, are explained in the glossary.

TIMELINE
2010 – The timeline shows you when important discoveries and inventions were made.

BEFORE SUBMARINES

Submarines are special boats that travel underwater. Before submarines were invented, people did not know much about the world deep below the ocean's surface. They dived in shallow water to explore and to find things such as shells and treasure.

People need to breathe in **oxygen** from air to stay alive. Divers held their breath or carried sacks full of air underwater. The air did not last long, which meant divers needed to return to the surface often to breathe in more air. People could stay underwater longer when they carried on breathing in air from the surface through hollow reeds, which were like straws. These were the first **snorkels**.

Divers with snorkels can only breathe underwater when they are close to the surface.

● **around 3000 BC** – Greek divers use hollow straws to breathe while underwater

3000 BC　　　　　2000 BC　　　　　1000 BC

Diving bells

Diving bells were heavy containers made of metal, wood, or glass that people used to go underwater. An object floats in water when the upwards push on it from the water (called **upthrust**) is greater than the downwards force of the object's weight. Diving bells sank because the downwards force of their weight was greater than the upthrust. The bell trapped a big bubble of air so people inside it could breathe.

 Here a diving bell helps people to find items from a shipwreck in 1752.

EUREKA!

The Greek king Alexander the Great used a glass diving bell in 332 BC. There is a legend that he saw a sea monster that was so big it took days to swim past the bell!

332 BC – Alexander the Great uses a diving bell

1578 – William Bourne publishes a book called *Inventions or Devices*. It contains his ideas for how to make a working submarine.

THE FIRST SUBMARINES

It took the efforts of many different inventors over hundreds of years to develop the submarines we know today. One of the earliest problems inventors solved was making a submarine **watertight**. If water filled the submarine, the people inside it might drown.

The *Drebbel*

Cornelis Drebbel invented the first submarine in 1620. People thought it looked like two wooden rowing boats, one stuck on top of the other. It had a short tower on top, with a door for people to get in and out. People inside rowed the machine along using oars through the sides. The whole machine was covered with greased leather to stop water getting in any gaps, but it was probably still rather damp inside.

This is a model of the *Drebbel*. It was similar in shape to some modern submarines, but it would have been far less comfortable inside.

EUREKA!

Drebbel continued to improve his inventions. His third submarine was his biggest. Thousands of people stood on the banks of the River Thames in London when Drebbel's amazing submarine took its first public voyage in 1623. The submarine slowly carried along 16 passengers a few metres below the river's surface. It stayed underwater for about three hours.

1620 – The *Drebbel* is the first successful submarine

1600   1610   1620

Cornelis Drebbel (1572–1633)

Cornelis Drebbel was a Dutch inventor who worked for King James I of England. He used ideas of the British inventor William Bourne to help invent his successful submarine. As well as his submarine, Drebbel invented many other things, including a microscope and a machine that told the time, date, and season.

1634 – A French priest and scientist called Marin Mersenne writes that submarines should be made of copper and shaped like long cylinders to move easily through the water

Ups and downs

Drebbel is said to have put heavy weights inside his submarine to make it sink. Making an object heavier in relation to its size or **volume** increases its **density**. There is more **upthrust** on a hollow metal boat than on a solid ball of metal of the same weight because its density is lower. Drebbel could only make his submarine rise by getting rid of the weights to lower its density.

In 1680, Italian inventor Giovanni Borelli invented **ballast tanks** so his submarine could rise and fall. He wrote about filling goatskin bags inside the submarine with water from outside to increase the submarine's density and make it sink. Then the water would be squeezed out of the bags to lower the submarine's density and make it rise.

This drawing from 1683 shows the ballast tanks inside Borelli's submarine.

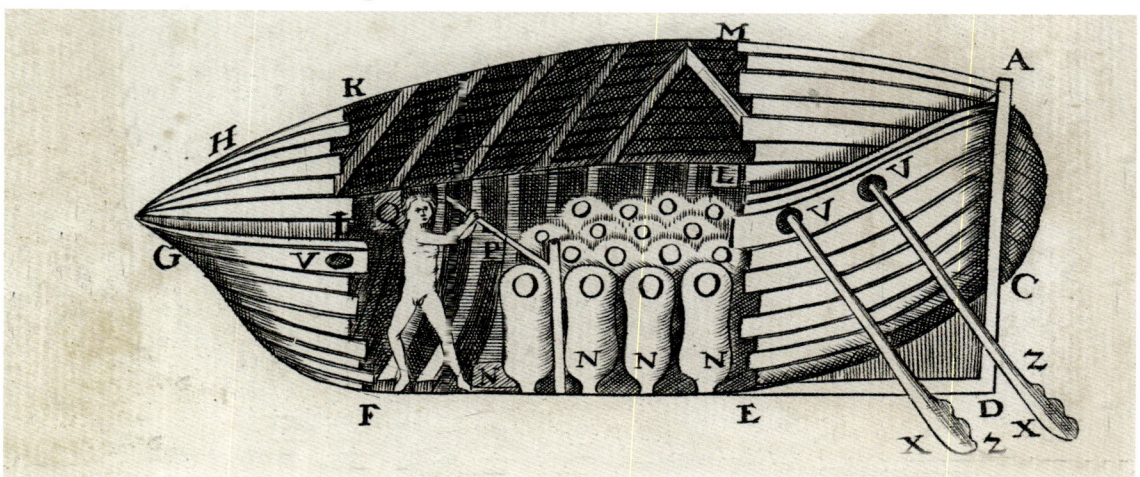

1653 – The *Rotterdam Boat* is invented but never works

1640　　　　　　1650　　　　　　1660

The carpenter's submarine

The English carpenter Nathaniel Symons invented a submarine with a changing volume in 1729. He sat inside and turned a handle to pull the two halves of the submarine together or spread them apart. When the halves were spread apart, the submarine rose up in the water because it had a bigger volume, and so it was less dense. When the halves were pushed together again, the submarine sank because it had a smaller volume and a greater density.

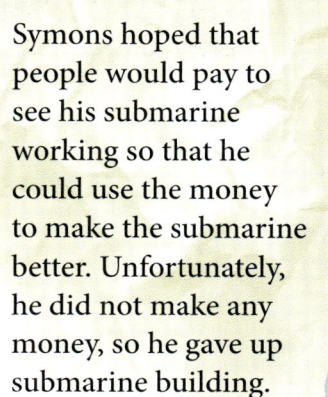

Setbacks

Symons hoped that people would pay to see his submarine working so that he could use the money to make the submarine better. Unfortunately, he did not make any money, so he gave up submarine building.

FLOATS
biggest volume
lowest density

SINKS
smallest volume
highest density

weight
upthrust
weight
upthrust

The red arrows in this diagram show how a submarine's volume affects how much upthrust is pushing on it and whether the submarine sinks or rises in the water, even though its weight stays the same.

Sneaking up on the enemy

As submarines improved, governments of different countries realized they could use them to sneak up and attack their enemies. In 1653, the French inventor De Son made the *Rotterdam Boat* for the Belgian navy. They planned to use it to ram holes in British navy ships. Unfortunately, it was too heavy to be moved by the sailors inside it!

The *Rotterdam Boat* was the first submarine designed to attack enemy warships, such as these.

1680 – Giovanni Borelli invents the ballast tank to change the weight and **density** of a submarine

1680   1690   1700

The *Turtle*

The *Turtle* was the first submarine to attack an enemy warship. This wooden, egg-shaped machine was invented by the American David Bushnell in 1776, during the American Revolution. The *Turtle* could move underwater towards enemy British ships, drill holes in their bottoms, and attach clockwork **mines** to blow them up.

It was very cramped inside the *Turtle* submarine. There were handles and foot pedals to spin the **propellers**, move the **rudder** outside, and to fill or empty the **ballast tanks**. Because it was such hard work to operate everything at once, the *Turtle* could only move very slowly.

The *Turtle* got its name because its curved shape looked like a turtle's shell. This 1776 illustration shows what it looked like inside.

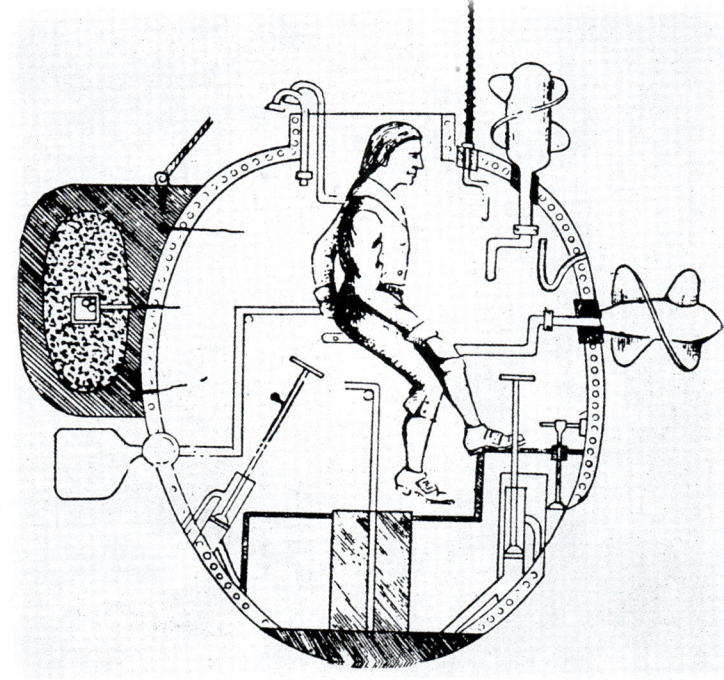

Setbacks

On 6 September 1776, Sergeant Lee, an American, moved the *Turtle* next to a British ship called the *Eagle* in New York harbour. He tried to drill a hole in the ship but failed to attach the mine. Lee ran out of air and had to come to the surface, where the enemy chased him off.

IMPROVING SUBMARINES

When a submarine moves through water, **drag** slows it down. Drag is the push of water you can feel when you swim in a pool. A submarine can move faster if it has a smooth, **streamlined** shape because water flows more easily past it, reducing the amount of drag.

The *Nautilus*

In 1797, Robert Fulton designed a new submarine with a streamlined, metal body that would allow it to attack enemies faster. The *Nautilus* had a sail so that it could use wind to move on the water's surface. The sail folded down once the *Nautilus* dived so it did not increase drag underwater. To move underwater, a handle was turned on the inside to work a **propeller** outside.

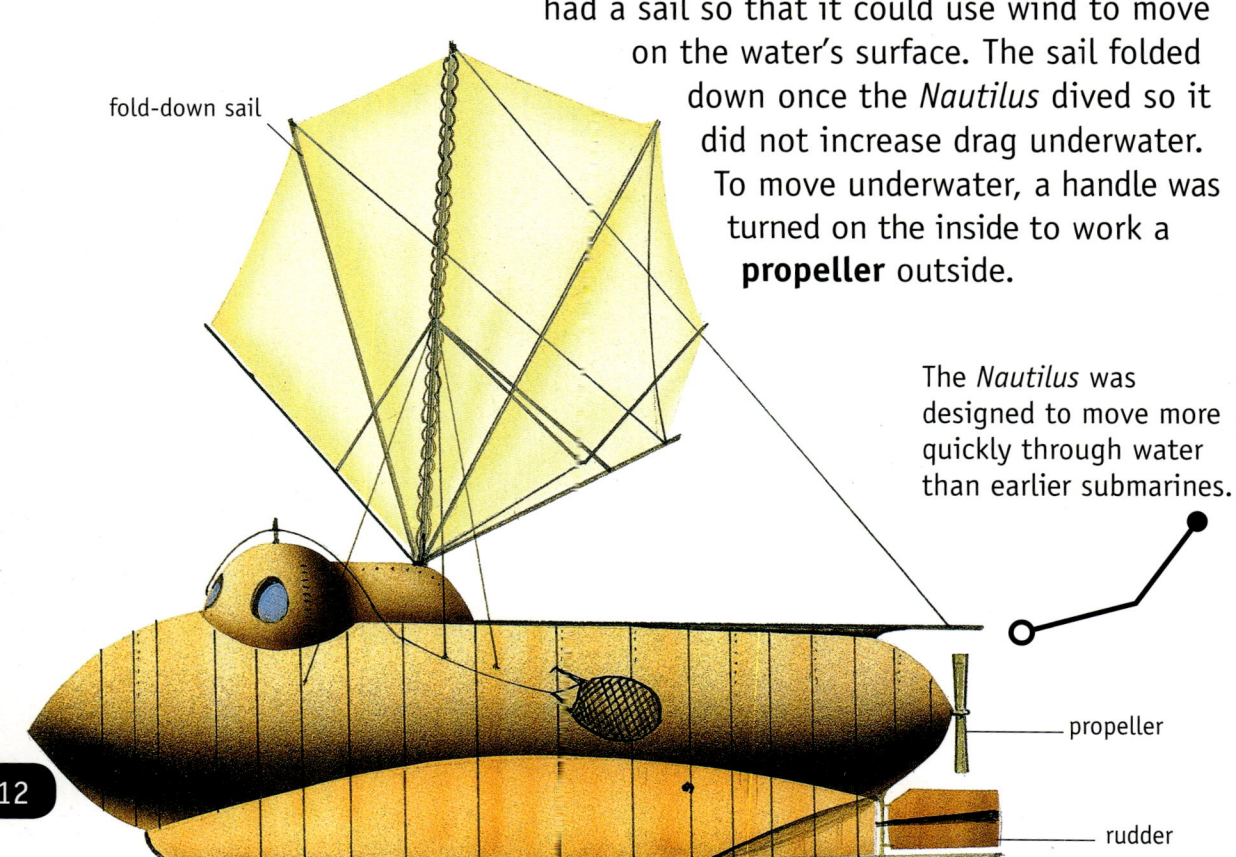

fold-down sail

The *Nautilus* was designed to move more quickly through water than earlier submarines.

propeller

rudder

1729 – Nathaniel Symons builds a submarine that can change its **volume**

1720   1730   1740

Robert Fulton (1765–1815)

American artist Robert Fulton was only a teenager when he made paddle wheels to move a fishing boat on water. Soon he became fascinated by the idea of a "plunging boat". In 1800, Fulton paid to have the *Nautilus* built. He hoped the French government would buy it to use in their war against Britain. The French first thought fighting with submarines was cowardly, but they were impressed with Fulton's submarine in trials. When the *Nautilus* was used in a real attack, it was too slow to catch a British ship. Fulton broke his submarine up and moved on to inventing steamships instead.

Breathing problems

When we breathe in air to get **oxygen**, we breathe out **carbon dioxide**. This gas is poisonous if you breathe too much in. The first submarines could not stay underwater for long because carbon dioxide built up inside them. They could only stay underwater for a long time if the submarine stayed near the surface so the crew could take in fresh air through **snorkels**.

In 1861, Brutus de Villeroi invented the USS *Alligator*. This was the first submarine with a system for keeping the air fresh. Pumping air through a bottle of special liquid removed the carbon dioxide.

The USS *Alligator* was 4 metres (47 feet) long. Like today's submarines, it had a **streamlined** shape and an air-cleaning system.

1776 – David Bushnell invents and demonstrates his *Turtle* submarine

1760   1770   1780

Setbacks

The USS *Alligator* was launched in 1862. Unfortunately, its air-cleaning system did not work well, so the crew also had to take tanks of fresh air on board to breathe.

Weapon of war

During the American Civil War (1861–1865), one side offered money to submarine inventors who could sink enemy navy ships. The *H.L. Hunley* submarine, named after the man who paid for it, sank the USS *Housatonic* in 1864 by ramming an explosive harpoon into its side. After this success the *H.L. Hunley* also sank, but nobody knows why.

This illustration shows the inside of the *H.L. Hunley*. The crew of eight turned the **propeller** fast enough to ram enemy ships.

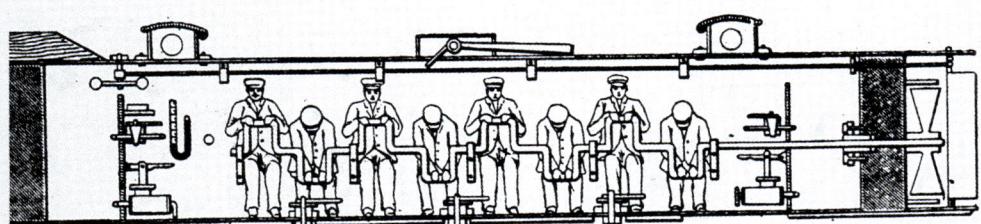
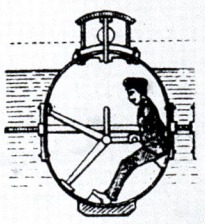

1797 – Robert Fulton invents the *Nautilus*

1790　　　　　　　　1800

SUBMARINES WITH ENGINES

Objects move forwards through water when the **thrust** (the force moving them forwards) is stronger than the **drag**. Early submarines were slow because sailors could not turn the **propellers** fast enough to create a strong thrust. This changed when people invented engines to create more thrust. Today, powerful engines turn giant propellers to thrust submarines fast through the water.

Air power

The *Diver*, invented in 1863 by Charles Burn and Simon Bourgeois, was the first submarine with an engine. The engine used **compressed air**, which is air forced into a small space, for power. Air moved fast from air tanks into a tube-shaped cylinder. This pushed on a piston (a type of plunger) inside. When the piston moved, it turned a **crankshaft** connected to a propeller. The engine had several cylinders with pistons that together spun the propeller fast.

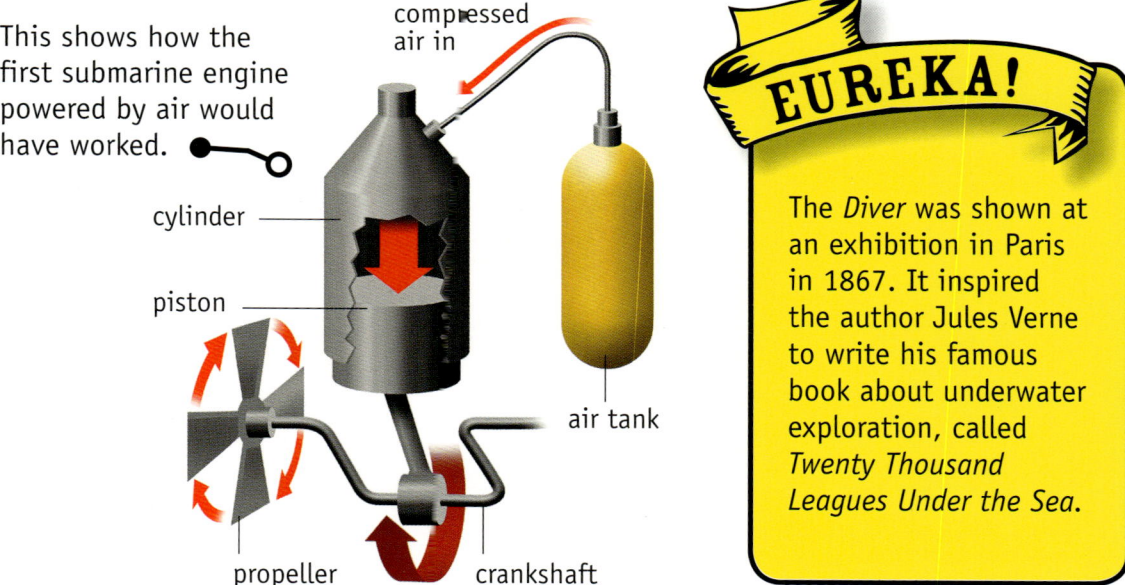

This shows how the first submarine engine powered by air would have worked.

compressed air in
cylinder
piston
air tank
propeller
crankshaft

EUREKA!

The *Diver* was shown at an exhibition in Paris in 1867. It inspired the author Jules Verne to write his famous book about underwater exploration, called *Twenty Thousand Leagues Under the Sea*.

The first torpedoes

In 1866, Robert Whitehead invented **torpedoes**. These are underwater weapons that allow submarines to attack enemies safely from a distance. The first torpedoes were long tubes packed with explosives. They had compressed air inside that thrust them forwards when it was released. Today, torpedoes have engines inside them and they can steer themselves towards their targets.

This illustration shows a modern submarine launching a torpedo.

Electric submarine

In a **steam engine**, coal is burned to heat water. The hot water produces steam that moves pistons and turns wheels or **propellers**. People found that it was not good to use steam engines inside submarines because burning coal used up the **oxygen** that sailors needed to breathe, and made lots of heat and smoke.

In 1897, John Philip Holland invented the *Holland VI* submarine, which used **battery** power. A battery is a store of electricity. Electricity from the batteries made an electric motor turn the propeller. The *Holland VI* also had an engine that burned petrol to power the propeller. Sailors ran this engine when the submarine was near the surface to move the submarine and to recharge its batteries.

This *Holland VI* submarine belonged to the US Navy.

1852 – Lodner Phillips invents a submarine propeller that can angle to steer the machine

1862 – The USS *Alligator* is the longest, most advanced submarine in the world

1840　　　　　1850　　　　　1860

John Philip Holland (1840-1914)

John Philip Holland was an Irish schoolteacher who spent half his life inventing submarines. His sixth submarine, the *Holland VI*, was the most successful. It held six sailors and could travel 50 kilometres (30 miles) underwater before the batteries needed to be recharged. The submarine could stay underwater for 40 hours but it was very cramped onboard. Holland sold many bigger and faster versions of the *Holland VI* to the British, Japanese, Russian, and United States navies. One of Holland's last inventions was a machine designed to help sailors escape from damaged submarines.

1863 – The *Diver* is the first submarine with an engine, powered by **compressed air**

1864 – The Spanish submarine *Ictineo II* is the first submarine to use steam power at the surface and a different chemical engine underwater

1864 – The *H.L. Hunley* is successfully used in the American Civil War

1866 – Robert Whitehead invents the **torpedo**

1870   1880

Nuclear submarines

During World War I (1914–1918) and World War II (1939–1945) all submarines used electric motors. In 1954, the United States Navy launched the first nuclear submarine. The *Nautilus* had a **steam engine**, but the heat to make the steam came from a **nuclear reactor**. This is a sealed container filled with special metals that keep releasing heat for years.

Nuclear submarines could go faster and further than electric ones. They did not need to come to the surface to recharge **batteries** or return to land to get more fuel. The trouble with nuclear reactors is that they are very expensive and dangerous if they go wrong. Today, most big navy submarines are nuclear, but many smaller submarines are still electric.

Here, a nuclear submarine surfaces through Arctic sea ice.

In 1958, the *Nautilus* became the first submarine to travel under the thick sea ice of the North Pole, from the Atlantic to the Pacific Oceans. The submarine stayed underwater without surfacing for a distance of about 3,000 kilometres (1,800 miles).

1897 – John Holland builds the petrol and electric *Holland VI*

1880   1890   1900

Submarine comforts

Modern nuclear submarines can weigh more than 24,000 tonnes (23,500 tons) – as much as 200 blue whales – and can carry 150 sailors. They are much more comfortable for sailors to live in than earlier submarines. They have bedrooms, showers and toilets, and a restaurant open 24 hours a day. They have special machines to turn seawater into drinking water and to keep the air fresh.

These crewmen are relaxing in the cramped spaces of the nuclear submarine NR-1.

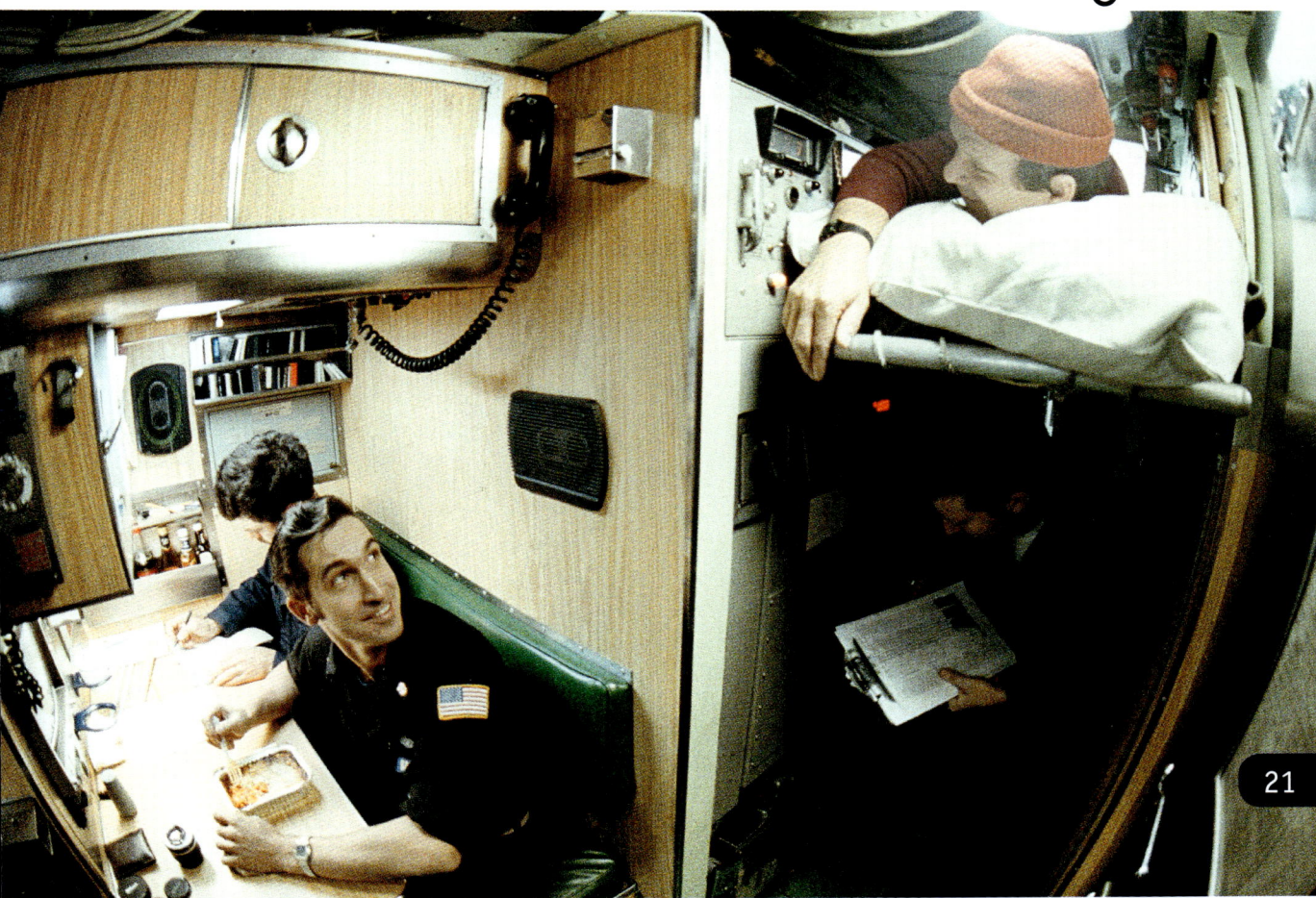

1902 – Simon Lake invents the modern submarine **periscope**

1910   1920

EXPLORING THE OCEANS

The deeper a submarine goes underwater, the more water there is above it. The weight of this water pressing down is called **water pressure**. To go really deep underwater, inventors had to make submarines to survive the enormous water pressure there.

Water pressure at a few tens of metres deep could force in water through gaps in the **hulls** of early submarines. Their hulls could collapse and windows could crack. Many of today's submarines have hulls made of very strong steel that is more than 15 centimetres (6 inches) thick, and windows made of even thicker glass or plastic. Now submarines can dive hundreds of metres deep into the ocean.

Here, the Mir2 is about to reach the Mid-Atlantic Ridge, on the bottom of the Atlantic Ocean.

Here, the *Trieste* is being lowered into the sea.

The deepest submarine

Only seven submarines with people inside have ever dived deeper than 3 kilometres (1.8 miles). In 1960 the *Trieste*, invented by Auguste Piccard, went down to almost 11 kilometres (7 miles) deep. The people inside sat in a small metal sphere that was part of the hull. This shape is best at coping with high water pressure, which at that depth was like having 50 jumbo jets sitting on top of the submarine!

EUREKA!

In January 1960, Jacques Piccard and Donald Walsh reached the bottom of the Marianas Trench near the Phillipines in the *Trieste*. The trench is the deepest point of all the oceans.

1948 – Hyman Rickover develops a small **nuclear reactor** that is designed to power a submarine

1953 – Dimitri Rebikoff invents the first **ROV** submarine

1954 – USS *Nautilus* is the first nuclear submarine

1950

1960

Looking above

From inside a submarine, sailors can look above the water for enemy ships by using a **periscope**. Periscopes are long tubes with angled mirrors inside. Light from the outside hits the top mirror, reflects down through the periscope, and off the lower mirror.

Early periscopes were not very good. In 1902, American inventor Simon Lake created a better version with **lenses** inside. Lenses are discs of glass that help to enlarge and focus what sailors can see through a periscope. The periscopes on today's nuclear submarines have digital cameras that can show the view on a computer screen.

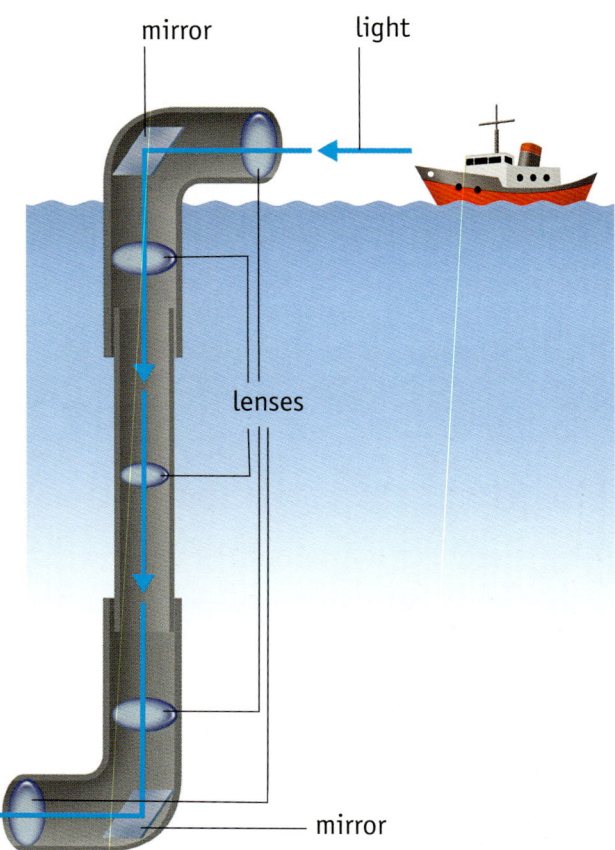

This diagram shows how a periscope is used for looking above the surface of the water.

1960 – The *Trieste* carries out the deepest manned dive in history

1964 – The magnetic sea engine is invented

1981 – The first Typhoon class nuclear submarine, the biggest ever submarine, is launched by the Russian Navy

1960　　　　1970　　　　1980

Submarines without people

In 1953, an inventor called Dimitri Rebikoff made the first robot submarine. It was called POODLE and did not need people on board to control it. Rebikoff operated his machine by sending computer instructions along a cable from a ship on the surface. Machines such as this are called Remote Operated Vehicles (**ROVs**). ROVs are usually small so they can explore shipwrecks and other places that larger submarines cannot.

EUREKA!

In 1986, Robert Ballard used the ROV *Jason Jr.* to take the first photographs inside the world's most famous shipwreck, the *Titanic*. This ship sank to the bottom of the Atlantic Ocean after crashing into an iceberg in 1912.

Here, ROV *Jason Jr.* can be seen exploring the *Titanic* shipwreck.

1986 – ROV *Jason Jr.* takes the first photographs inside the *Titanic* shipwreck

1990   2000

INTO THE FUTURE

Submarines have changed a lot since they were first invented 400 years ago. Today submarines are bigger, more **streamlined**, and faster. They can dive deeper, travel further, and stay underwater longer. In what ways could submarines change in the future?

Some modern submarines are massive. Here, the newly built HMS *Astute* submarine is being transported to the sea.

No propellers

In the future, submarines may move around without **propellers**. Some may pump jets of water backwards to make themselves **thrust** forwards. Others may use special **magnets** to make a jet of water thrust them forwards. In 2007, James Tangorra invented a robot fish fin that could make an **ROV** thrust forwards, change direction, and also hover on the spot. It uses less electricity than propellers.

2004 – Rob Innes builds the *Seabreacher* submarine

2008 – The *Super Falcon* submarine is launched

2000　　　　　　　　　2010　　　　　　　　　2020

Underwater tourism

The *Super Falcon* submarine, invented by Graham Hawkes in 2008, is built for two people. It is shaped like a small fighter aircraft. It is light, fast, and has long wings that help it to dive. On some coasts, such as those in Hawaii in the United States, there are already large submarines that take tourists on trips underwater. In future, tourists may stay at underwater hotels and explore the oceans in their own personal submarines like the *Super Falcon*.

The *Seabreacher* personal submarine can roll and even leap out of the water.

EUREKA!

Keen surfer Thomas Rowe designed a robot dolphin submarine after watching dolphins playing in the waves. His student Rob Innes later built the *Seabreacher* submarine based on Rowe's designs.

TIMELINE

3000 BC — Greek divers use hollow straws to breathe while underwater

332 BC — Alexander the Great uses a diving bell

1578 — William Bourne publishes a book called *Inventions and Devices*. It contains his ideas for how to make a working submarine.

1797 — Robert Fulton invents the *Nautilus*

1852 — Lodner Phillips invents a submarine **propeller** that can angle to steer the machine

1862 — The USS *Alligator* is the longest, most advanced submarine in the world

1863 — The *Diver* is the first submarine with an engine, powered by **compressed air**

1864 — The Spanish submarine *Ictineo II* is the first steam-powered submarine

1864 — The *H.L. Hunley* is successfully used in the American Civil War

1866 — Robert Whitehead invents the **torpedo**

1981 — The first Typhoon class nuclear submarine, the biggest ever submarine, is launched by the Russian Navy

1986 — ROV *Jason Jr.* takes the first photographs inside the *Titanic* shipwreck

2004 — Rob Innes builds the *Seabreacher* submarine

2008 — The *Super Falcon* submarine is launched

28

1620
The *Drebbel* is the world's first successful submarine

1634
A French priest and scientist called Marin Mersenne writes that submarines should be made of copper and shaped like long cylinders to move easily through the water

1653
The *Rotterdam Boat* is invented but never works

1776
David Bushnell invents and demonstrates his *Turtle* submarine. It is the first submarine able to move independently above and below the water

1729
Nathaniel Symons builds a submarine that can change its **volume**

1680
Giovanni Borelli invents the **ballast tank** to change the weight and **density** of a submarine

1897
John Philip Holland builds the petrol and electric *Holland VI*

1902
Simon Lake invents the modern submarine **periscope**

1948
Hyman Rickover develops a small **nuclear reactor** to power a submarine

1964
The magnetic sea engine is invented

1960
The *Trieste* carries out the deepest manned dive in history

1954
USS *Nautilus* is the first nuclear submarine

1953
Dimitri Rebikoff invents the first **ROV** submarine

GLOSSARY

ballast tank compartment in a submarine that can fill with water or empty to make it sink or float

battery device storing chemicals that produce electricity

carbon dioxide gas in air that living things breathe out, or that is produced by burning fuels

compressed air air reduced in volume and increased in pressure. Bicycle tyres stay firm because they are filled with compressed air.

crankshaft shaft that turns when engine pistons move up and down

density how heavy something is for its size, or volume

drag force acting against the movement of a person, animal, or vehicle

hull frame or body of a submarine or boat

lens glass or plastic object that makes an image clearer or bigger

magnet piece of metal that attracts metal objects towards it

mine type of hidden bomb. Most mines explode when something touches them.

nuclear reactor machine to control the release of energy from special metals

oxygen gas in air that living things need to breathe in

periscope device shaped like a tube that allows someone to see over the top of something else

propeller device with two or more blades that pushes through water when it spins

ROV short for Remote Operated underwater Vehicle; robot submarine without people on board that is operated from a distance

rudder device to control the direction a submarine or ship moves in

snorkel tube to breathe in air from the surface while underwater, or a tube on a submarine letting air in and exhaust gases out from a working engine

steam engine engine that produces steam to move parts, usually by burning fuel such as coal

streamlined having a smooth, even shape to move easily and quickly through water

thrust force pushing a vehicle. A submarine has an engine and propeller to create thrust through water

torpedo long, narrow bomb fired underwater, usually from a submarine

upthrust upward pushing force acting on an object in water

volume amount of space that something takes up

water pressure push caused by the weight of water

watertight not letting any water leak in

FIND OUT MORE

Books

Bushnell's Submarine: The Best Kept Secret of the American Revolution, Arthur S. Lefkowitz (Scholastic, 2006)

Great Inventions: Submarines, Rebecca Stefoff (Marshall Cavendish, 2006)

How It Works: Ships and Submarines, Steve Parker (Miles Kelly Publishing, 2009)

Machines Close-up: Modern Warships and Submarines, Daniel Gilpin (Wayland, 2009)

Websites

Take a virtual tour of a submarine at:
www.njnm.com/LingInteractive/ling.html

Find out more about life on a submarine at:
americanhistory.si.edu/Subs/operating/aboard/index.html

Discover more about the *Seabreacher* personal submarine at:
www.seabreacher.com

Places to visit

Royal Navy Submarine Museum
Gosport, Hampshire PO12 2AS
www.rnsubmus.co.uk

The U-Boat Story exhibit
Birkenhead, Merseyside CH41 6DU
www.u-boatstory.co.uk

INDEX

air cleaning systems 14, 15, 21
Alexander the Great 5

Ballard, Robert 25
ballast tanks 8, 11
batteries 18, 19
Borelli, Giovanni 8
Bourgeois, Simon 16
Bourne, William 6, 7
Burn, Charles 16
Bushnell, David 11

carbon dioxide 14, 15
compressed air 16, 17
crankshafts 16

De Son 10
deepest dives 22–23
density 8, 9
Diver 16
divers 4
diving bells 5
drag 12, 16
Drebbel 6
Drebbel, Cornelis 6, 7, 8

electricity 18, 26
engines 16, 17, 18, 20, 26

first submarines 6–11
Fulton, Robert 12, 13

Hawkes, Graham 27
H.L. Hunley 15
Holland, John Philip 18, 19
Holland VI 18, 19
hulls 22

Ictineo II 18
Innes, Rob 27

Lake, Simon 24
lenses 24

magnets 26
Mersenne, Marin 7
mines 11

Nautilus (early submarine) 12, 13
Nautilus (nuclear submarine) 20
North Pole 20
nuclear reactors 20
nuclear submarines 20–21, 24

oxygen 4, 14, 18

periscopes 24
personal submarines 27
Phillips, Lodner 14
Piccard, Auguste 23
pistons 16, 18
propellers 11, 12, 14, 15, 16, 18, 26

Rebikoff, Dimitri 25
Remote Operated Vehicles (ROVs) 25, 26
Rickover, Hyman 20
robot submarines 25
Rotterdam Boat 10
Rowe, Thomas 27
rudders 11

Seabreacher 27
snorkels 4, 14
steam engines 18, 20
streamlined shape 12, 14, 26
Super Falcon 27
Symons, Nathaniel 9

Tangorra, James 26
thrust 16, 26
Titanic 25
torpedoes 17
Trieste 23
Turtle 11
Typhoon class 21

upthrust 5, 8
USS Alligator 14, 15

Verne, Jules 16
Villeroi, Brutus de 15
volume 8, 9

warfare 10–11, 13, 15, 17
water pressure 22, 23
watertight 6
Whitehead, Robert 17